KEEPING SAFE

Volume 4

BESS COLLYER

GROLIER
EDUCATIONAL

about this set

Volume by volume, BEING HUMAN describes and illustrates the workings of the human body and mind, and explains how we behave as individuals and interact with the world in which we live. The set provides a wide-ranging introduction to human biology, psychology, sociology, and health and safety. It will help the reader understand the reasons for many of the things that we do—both as individuals and when part of a group—and will provide a fascinating yet sound basis for improving knowledge, life skills, and self-confidence.

There are eight volumes in the set:

Volume 1 – The Human Body;
Volume 2 – The Brain and Senses;
Volume 3 – Health and Illness;
Volume 4 – Keeping Safe;
Volume 5 – Personality and
        Behavior;

Volume 6 – Communication;
Volume 7 – Relationships;
Volume 8 – The Human Race.

Although each volume deals with a different subject, many of them are interrelated, and the student will find the cross-references to other volumes in the set an invaluable way of discovering more information about topics.

Throughout the set there are numerous high-quality color photographs, charts, and diagrams that illustrate many of the topics under discussion. A special feature of the set is the inclusion of projects and other activities in each volume that will enable the reader to discover more about himself or herself at first hand. Each volume also contains a useful glossary explaining many of the words used in the text and an index to all the volumes in the set.

PUBLISHED 2000 BY
Grolier Educational, Danbury, CT 06816
This edition published exclusively for
the school and library market

PLANNED AND PRODUCED BY
Andromeda Oxford Limited,
11–13 The Vineyard,
Abingdon, Oxon OX14 3PX, UK

EDITED AND DESIGNED BY
Derek Hall & Associates

Set ISBN 0-7172-9419-6
Volume 4 ISBN 0-7172-9423-4

Library of Congress Cataloging-in-Publication Data
Being human/edited by Derek Hall.
   p. cm.
   ISBN 0-7172-9419-6 (set)
    1. Human beings- -Juvenile literature.
I. Hall, Derek, 1930-

   GN31.5.S73 1999

                              99–034157

Printed in Hong Kong

EDITORIAL CONSULTANTS
John Clark
Dr. Poppy Nash
Dr. John Wright

ILLUSTRATIONS
Julian Baker
Ruth Lindsay
Richard Orr/Bernard Thornton Artists

PHOTOGRAPHIC ACKNOWLEDGMENTS
4 St John Ambulance; **5** ISI/Allsport; **6**
Robert Harding Picture Library/Adam
Woolfitt; **7** Sally Greenhill; **8** The Stock
Market/Ronnie Kaufman; **10** The Stock
Market; **11** Sally and Richard Greenhill;
12 ISI; **13** Richard Greenhill; **14** The
Stock Market/Richard Abarno; **16** (top)
ISI; **16** (bottom) The Stock Market; **17**
Sam Greenhill; **18** The Stock
Market/Ronnie Kaufman; **19** Derek Hall
and Associates; **20** ISI; **22** Derek Hall and
Associates; **23** Derek Hall and Associates;
24 Robert Harding Picture Library; **25**
The Stock Market/Michael Heron; **cover
pictures:** (top left) Science Photo
Library/Ralph Eagle; (bottom left)
Science Photo Library/Andrew
McClenaghan; (top right) Sally Greenhill;
(bottom right) The Stock Market.

ISI – Chris Fairclough at Image Select
International, except page 5.

*While every effort has been made to
trace the copyright holders of illustrations in this book, the publishers will be
pleased to rectify any omissions or
inaccuracies.*

CONTENTS

INTRODUCTION

KEEPING SAFE MEANS avoiding dangers in our everyday lives. Sometimes, we can do this by being sensible and thoughtful and knowing about possibly dangerous situations that we might encounter. Keeping safe is also about protecting and caring for others, and this may also involve the use of the rescue and first-aid techniques described in this book that could even save a life.

This book describes many of the methods you can use to ensure you keep safe, healthy, and out of danger at home, at school, or when traveling.

It also provides valuable information about how to care for others by giving simple first aid or by helping them get comfortable when they are unwell or injured. There is also advice here about how you can learn more about first aid—it could even help you save a life.

Keeping safe means many different things. First, it means knowing which situations are likely to be dangerous and how to avoid them. This often requires nothing more than using common sense and thinking through the consequences of your actions before you do something. (For instance, it might be better to avoid swimming in a river until you have checked out the strength of the current or asked someone who is knowledgeable about the area if it is safe to swim there.)

Second, it means knowing how to deal with unexpected problems if they do occur—and

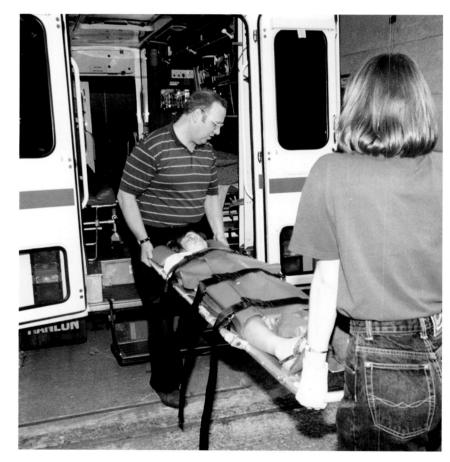

that includes knowing how to get the right sort of help. This book will show you many of the things you can do to keep safe in what otherwise might become potentially dangerous situations.

Special Training

People who join the volunteer emergency services are highly trained in all aspects of first aid and life-saving. These volunteers (above) are learning to use ambulance equipment.

We begin by looking at personal safety (pages 6-7) and then go on to consider safety in the home and yard (pages 8-9), including the safety of other family members like younger brothers and sisters. The many ways we use to travel—both at home and abroad—can sometimes be potentially hazardous, and advice is also given on how to travel safely and on how to maintain bicycles (see pages 10-11).

Being safe at school involves knowing about rules designed for safety as well as knowing how to avoid harmful substances (see pages 12-13). Many of the harmful substances we may be offered, and the effects that they can have on our bodies, are described on pages 14-15.

Between pages 16 and 23 we look at the various places we visit, including when we are on vacation. There is advice about keeping safe in cities, on country walks and trips, and when near water—including how to avoid dangerous animals. Pages 24 and 25 describe what to do in emergencies and, most importantly, how to get help.

Finally, pages 28-37 describe a range of common illnesses, injuries, and everyday aches and pains, and give advice on how they can be treated.

Learning First Aid

There are some very simple first-aid tips described in this book that you can easily apply yourself—such as how to make someone who has a toothache more comfortable. However, there are others—like giving a victim mouth-to-mouth resuscitation—that are included to show what an experienced first aider will do in an emergency situation. Do not attempt any technique if you feel unsure how to apply it properly.

If you are interested in learning more about first aid so that you can provide life-saving care if necessary, there are organizations that offer training. Having sound, thorough knowledge of such techniques is invaluable.

Safety in Sports

Some very physical contact sports, like football (right) and ice hockey, could cause injury if the players were not protected with padding and helmets. It is always advisable to wear the recommended clothing in any sport.

PERSONAL SAFETY

YOUR PERSONAL SAFETY is your own responsibility. We learn much about being safe from our parents or other caregivers when we are young, but as we grow older, we face situations in which we must sometimes look after ourselves. Some of the more specific issues about safety are to be found in other parts of this book, but here we deal with the basic aspects of keeping safe in everyday life.

Throughout this volume there is advice and information about ways to keep safe when you are in particular places or doing particular things, or when you are faced with emergencies or unforeseen situations. Here, however, we look at ways in which you can help ensure your personal safety as you go about your everyday life. We also look at ways in which you can help protect your personal belongings.

Playing Safely

If you cannot play in the safety of a yard, the park, or in the house, let your parents or caregivers know where you are going. Do not play near roads or railways. You should also avoid places like old quarries (which can be dangerous due to the possibility of falling rocks

or may be filled with deep water) and old buildings (which may be unsafe or may be frequented by drug users). Rivers and lakes can also be dangerous (see pages 20–21).

If you find any unusual objects while playing—canisters or unmarked bottles of liquid, for example—do not touch them, but inform your parents, caregivers, or the police.

Do not tease farm animals—which may feel threatened and attack you—or dogs, particularly if they are guarding property by standing at a gate, for example.

Avoiding Crime

You can do a lot to avoid crimes such as muggings by keeping away from places like poorly lit sidestreets and neighborhoods that are known to be

Avoiding Fights

Sometimes arguments or misunderstandings between people develop into fights (left). Do not involve yourself in other people's fights; just keep away. If you see someone being attacked or robbed, however, call the police.

checklist

Some personal safety tips:
- **Always tell someone where you are going and when you expect to return.**
- **Make sure you have your house keys and enough money to get home.**
- **Always refuse drugs.**
- **Avoid going with strangers.**
- **Be sure you know how to make an emergency telephone call.**
- **Don't carry valuables.**
- **Keep handbags and the like securely closed.**
- **Try to look confident.**
- **Remember that some places are best avoided. Don't wander off alone and get lost.**

dangerous. It is also advisable not to carry more money than you need. Do not put all your money or valuables in one pocket or bag. If you put coats or bags down in cafes or shops, keep an eye on them at all times. If you have a personal stereo, put it away out of sight when it is not in use.

Staying in touch is a good way to keep safe. As well as letting your parents or caregivers know where you are going, it is sensible to contact them to let them know you are safe and well—this is particularly important if you are traveling abroad (see page 11). It is also worthwhile informing them of any changes in your plans.

Looking Confident

At events like pop festivals (above) or in crowded streets, where you are mixing closely with a large number of people, try to look confident and relaxed. Keep jewelry, money, and items like personal stereos out of sight.

Your Health

Keeping your health safe is important, too, and the volume *Health and Illness* provides much advice about exercise, diet, and other health issues. Smog and other forms of pollution affect us more and more today, and if we can, we should try to avoid unhealthy places as well as unhealthy lifestyles.

SAFETY IN THE HOME AND YARD

ALTHOUGH OUR HOME is usually the place we feel safest, every year many thousands of accidents occur in the home or the yard—especially to young children and old people. Many of these accidents can be avoided if you are aware of the potential dangers.

Accidents usually happen because someone has been careless or has used something in a way it was not intended to be used. A little thought can prevent many mishaps from occurring. Family members should look after each other, and you should try to ensure older family members or younger sisters or brothers are not in danger. If an accident

Gun Safety

Guns intended for hunting or target shooting should only be used, outdoors or on specially designed firing ranges, by experienced or authorized persons. All guns should be locked securely away in gun cabinets when not in use. They should never be left loaded. Never point a gun at anyone as a joke or pull the trigger unless you are using the gun in an authorized manner. You should never take guns into schools or other public places. There are laws concerning the purchase and use of guns that vary from state to state. Your local police department or gun dealer will have details.

occurs at home, it may be you who must assist the victim or get help (see pages 24–25 and 28–37 in particular).

Falls account for many accidents in the home, so make sure toys and other items are not left where people might trip over them. If you spill liquids, wipe them up, since slippery floors can be dangerous.

Most households use substances that can cause poisoning. There may be bleach, detergents, solvents, and cleaners. Read the safety labels on the containers, and never allow

Helping Your Family

You can help the older members of your family—especially if they are infirm or confined to a wheelchair (above)—by making sure, for example, that everyday items they use are within easy reach.

these substances to enter the body (see page 9). Leave the substances in their original containers—never transfer them to a drink bottle. Any substance no longer required should be disposed of properly. Medicines must also only be used in accordance with the instructions provided. Keep all medicines away from young children.

If you smell gas in the home, do not turn any lights on or attempt to light the gas; open the window, and turn the gas off or get help. Fire can be a major hazard, and you should read the advice given on pages 26–27 concerning fire safety.

In the Yard

Playing in the yard can be safe and fun if you remember a few rules. In the same way that you should not leave things lying around the house, do not leave garden tools, bicycles, or other items where thay can cause an accident. Put things in their proper place when you have finished with them.

If you are allowed to use guns in the yard, make sure you fire them only at proper targets. Never use guns in a way that might injure other people, and never leave guns where young children can touch them.

Every year there are tragic and unnecessary deaths caused by children becoming locked inside discarded household items like freezers. These objects are dangerous and should not be used for play. Any unwanted household items such as these, as well as old furniture, bottles, and so on should be taken to the dump by a responsible adult.

Some plants are also poisonous. A few of the most common dangerous plants are shown below.

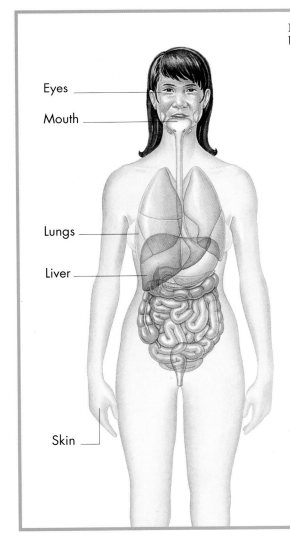

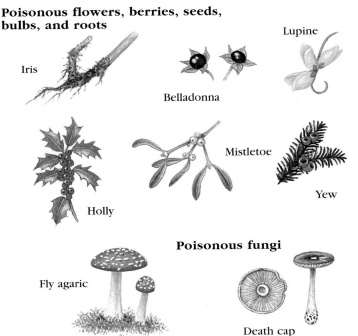

Poisonous flowers, berries, seeds, bulbs, and roots

Iris

Belladonna

Lupine

Holly

Mistletoe

Yew

Poisonous fungi

Fly agaric

Death cap

Poisons

Poisons can enter the body in a number of different ways. They can enter through the eyes; through the airway when we breathe; they can be injected; they can enter when an animal such as a snake bites; they can be swallowed; or in the case of some chemicals, they can be absorbed through the skin. Poisons may attack organs such as the liver or the lungs. Many cases of poisoning are the result of eating poisonous plants like those shown above. Do not put any plants in your mouth, and only touch those you know are safe.

TRAVEL SENSE

KEEPING SAFE WHEN we travel means observing a few simple rules. If you are walking, take extra care when near roads. If you are using a vehicle on public roads, be sure to observe the rules and bylaws. You must also ensure that your method of transport—whether it is a bicycle or a car—is in good working order. Do not use rollerblades, skateboards, and so on where they could be a danger to others.

One of the journeys you will take most often is the one to and from school. It may involve you walking all the way or walking to catch the school bus or a train. Remember that you are traveling at the same time as commuters, shoppers, and other travelers—many of whom will be in their cars rushing to their destinations. Take extra care at these busy times. Observe the traffic, and watch out for fast-approaching vehicles. If possible, cross streets at specially marked places, and obey "Walk" and "Don't Walk" signs.

Crossing the Road
Busy roads like this highway (above) jammed with rush-hour traffic need extra care. Only cross where it is safe to do so—such as by a bridge or an underpass.

Make sure saddle is correct height

Lubricate all moving parts

Check brake pads are free from dirt and not worn

Ensure chain is correctly tensioned and greased

Bicycle Maintenance
Keep your bicycle in a safe and roadworthy condition by following the maintenance instructions left. Make sure lights are working correctly.

Check tire condition and pressures and remove stones, etc.

If you use any sort of vehicle for travel, it should be maintained properly. On page 10 there is advice about how to maintain your bicycle, but even rollerblades, skateboards, and the like need to be looked after. Straps and fasteners need to be in good condition, and wheels and other moving parts must work efficiently. Not only will this make it safer for traveling, but it will also increase your enjoyment.

Cars need to be maintained correctly and driven safely. Brakes, steering, lights, and windshield wipers in particular must be in good working order. Seat belts and other safety devices like airbags should also be in good condition. Keep windshields clean.

Always drive carefully, particularly in places where people are likely to be around. Observe all speed limits, traffic signs, and other bylaws. If in doubt, get information from an experienced driver first.

Travel Abroad

When you travel abroad, there are many other things to remember. First, you may need a passport, visa, or other form of documentation to allow you to enter a foreign country. You must not stay in the country beyond the authorized date without getting official permission.

If you are going to spend any money, you may need some currency of the country you are visiting. It can be obtained from banks, currency exchanges, and so on. Many credit and charge cards can be used in foreign countries, too.

Some countries have laws controlling the kinds of things you can bring into, or out of, them. There may also be restrictions on the quantities of such items. This information is usually given on immigration forms or on posters at airports, ports, or border crossings.

You may also need to provide medical certificates giving proof of inoculation against certain diseases before you are allowed to enter some countries (see *Health and Illness*, page 9). If in doubt, seek advice from your doctor, from the travel company arranging your trip, or from the embassies of the countries you intend to visit.

Finally, never take drugs (see pages 14–15) into or out of a foreign country or accept any offers of drugs. Apart from the dangers from the drugs themselves, many countries—for example, some Asian countries—impose very severe penalties on anyone breaking their strict drug laws.

Using Skateboards

These boys (below) look confident on their skateboards, but it is advisable to wear helmets, gloves, and knee and elbow pads in case of a fall—particularly if you are an inexperienced skateboarder.

SAFETY AT SCHOOL

WE SPEND MUCH of our early lives at school, and it is important that we feel safe and secure there. Safety at school includes many different things. It means being safe from dangers outside the school, such as from drug dealers or people who might want to molest you, as well as being safe from dangers inside the school like bullies. Schools usually have some special rules designed to help keep you safe, too.

The first thing you may notice about your school is the fact that it is surrounded by a fence. This has several purposes: it helps keep the school secure from thieves and vandals when it is closed; it stops unauthorized persons entering the school during classes; and it prevents young schoolchildren from wandering off during breaks.

Although school should be a place where we feel safe and secure, there have been well-publicized incidents where guns, knives, and other weapons have been brought into schools by students with disastrous consequences. Many schools now search students before they enter the school to ensure they are not carrying such items in with them. Never bring weapons, drugs, or any other illegal or dangerous items into school.

If a student tries to sell you drugs at school, you should refuse them. If there is anyone loitering near the school trying to sell you drugs or other illegal

Early Learning

Learning about different aspects of safety usually begins at home and is continued at school. These young schoolchildren (below) are learning, through playing a game, that holding hands helps keep people together and safe.

things, you should report the incident to one of the teachers. You can find out more about the harmful effects of drugs on pages 14–15. The unhealthy effects of substances like tobacco and alcohol are described on pages 8–9 of *Health and Illness*.

You should also consider whether it is really necessary to bring valuable personal items into school. If you must, make sure they are kept secure.

Life at school is not just about learning subjects like math and English; it is also about learning how to interact with others—including learning how to deal with bullies and people who are trying to give you unwanted physical or sexual attention. Pages 16–17 of *Relationships* gives advice about what to do if you are being bullied. You should also tell a teacher if you are being given unwanted sexual attention.

Safety Rules

Some school rules are there to help you learn about discipline and respect for others, but many are designed to help keep you safe. Most schools have rules about wearing safety goggles and protective clothing, as well as taking other precautions, when working in classes such as science or technology. It is very important that you obey these rules. An accident caused by disregarding these precautions could injure you for life.

It is equally important not to play with chemicals or equipment, and never put yourself or others at risk through improper

use of any materials.

If you take part in sports at school, there may also be rules to ensure you use equipment safely. Many items of sports equipment—such as javelins or baseball bats—can cause injury to others if used incorrectly. Listen carefully to advice given by teachers or coaches. Remember also to exercise before sports to avoid sprains and other injuries.

Fire is a potential hazard in schools that must be taken very seriously. Your school will have its own fire drill (the procedure to be followed in case of fire), and you should pay attention during fire practice and remember what to do in case of fire (see also pages 26–27). If you discover a fire, alert a teacher or a senior pupil immediately.

Your school may also have other safety procedures to fol-

School Trips

You may go on a school trip at home or abroad. As well as following the advice given in this volume about travel, remember to look out for each other. Trips are often more fun, and safer, in the company of your schoolfriends (above).

low; remember, they are there for your protection, so learn them and follow them correctly.

Traveling with the School

Traveling with the school can be fun, but to avoid any dangers, ensure you heed all the advice given about the traveling arrangements and what sort of things you should take with you. Sometimes your school may give out special instruction sheets that need to be shown to your parents or caregivers.

HARMFUL SUBSTANCES

HARMFUL SUBSTANCES CAN be found in many places—in the back yard, in the garage, and even in the home. They include cleaning products, paint, fuels, and medicine. Many of these substances can cause damage to your health if used incorrectly or if swallowed or allowed to come into contact with other parts of the body. Other harmful substances include nonmedicinal, illegal drugs.

Cleaning products used in the home include ammonia and lye, which are poisonous and corrosive. Acids, such as sulfuric acid used in car batteries, are also corrosive. All of them should be stored in clearly labeled containers out of reach of small children.

Paints, as well as paint thinner and paint remover, are also poisonous. Fuels, such as gasoline, kerosene, and bottled gas, are highly flammable (likely to catch fire) as well as poisonous. They should be stored in a cool, safe place—such as a shed—away from the risk of fire.

Most medicines, especially those supplied as capsules or tablets, can be harmful if taken in large doses or by people for whom they were not prescribed. Even mild painkillers, such as aspirin and acetaminophen, can be dangerous. Aspirin should not be taken by anyone under the age of 12, even in small doses.

Illegal Drugs

Another hazard is the abuse of nonmedicinal drugs in our society. Some, such as alcohol and

tobacco, may be legally bought once you have reached a certain age. They are taken regularly by large numbers of people. But they are addictive and can cause serious illness, including heart disease and cancer (see *Health and Illness*, page 9). Even caffeine, found in coffee, tea, and cola drinks, can be harmful if taken in excess.

Alcohol is one of a class of drugs known as depressants. Others include barbiturates and tranquilizers. They have the effect of increasing the user's confidence and overcoming

Young Drug Users

Drug dealers, or pushers, know that taking some kinds of drugs can become habit-forming, or addictive, so they sell drugs to young people in order to get them addicted or "hooked" on drugs (above). In this way they gain new customers and a regular source of illegal money.

shyness. In large doses they can impair judgment and can cause drowsiness or sleep.

The opposite effects are caused by stimulant drugs. They include amphetamine and cocaine. They increase the heartbeat, giving a feeling of increased energy called a "high." Prolonged use can lead to physical and mental problems.

Narcotics include heroin and its derivatives. They cause drowsiness and a feeling of being remote from the real world. They depress breathing, and an overdose can kill. There are also various drugs, such as LSD, called hallucinogens. They distort the user's senses. Drugs like cocaine, heroine, and LSD are illegal in many countries. There can also be severe penalties for being caught in possession of drugs (see also page 11).

Drug Addiction

All of the drugs described above can rapidly lead to addiction. The user becomes physically dependent on the drug. Psychological dependence may also occur, in which the user needs regular doses of a drug in order to cope with everyday life. In either case, once a user is "hooked," it is extremely difficult to stop using the drug. Stopping may lead to distressing physical and mental withdrawal symptoms that range from depression and nightmares to attempting suicide (taking one's own life). Some drugs can be especially dangerous because they contain harmful additives. There is also a risk of infection from diseases such as AIDS or hepatitis (a disease of the liver) through the use of drugs.

The only guaranteed way to prevent drug addiction is to never start taking drugs. This can be difficult if other people around you are drinking or smoking or indulging in hard drugs. Fortunately, when most people become aware of how drugs can ruin lives, they have the good sense not to start.

Commonly Used Drugs

Caffeine—It is a stimulant drug found in coffee, tea, and cola drinks. Overuse of such drinks can cause excitement or sleeplessness.

Tobacco—It contains nicotine and tarry substances that can cause cancer, heart disease, and other illnesses. Its long-term use can eventually cause death.

Alcohol—Present in alcoholic drinks, it is actually a poison and a depressant. It makes people drunk and can be addictive. It can cause death.

Cannabis—It is made from the hemp plant (marijuana) and may be smoked as "dope" or eaten. It produces relaxation and talkativeness. It is not addictive, although long-term use may cause psychological dependence and problems with the lungs and the respiratory system.

Solvents—These are substances used in adhesives and aerosols that are abused by people sniffing them. They are fast-acting and extremely dangerous. They can cause death.

Amphetamines—Usually taken as tablets, and called "speed" or "bennies," these are stimulants, causing excitement and loss of appetite. Long-term use can cause depression and mental illness. A common type of amphetamine is "ecstacy" (see below).

Cocaine—Known as "coke" or "snow," it is usually sniffed in the form of a white powder. It causes brief feelings of power and well-being, but long-term use causes loss of appetite, sleeplessness, and mental problems. Its modern derivative is called "crack."

Opiates—These include opium, morphine, and heroin, or "smack." They are all derived from the milk of the opium poppy. Heroin comes in powder form and may be white, gray, brown, or beige. It may be sniffed, smoked, taken orally, or injected. Opiates produce a feeling of well-being and a relief from physical pain. Repeated use results in physical and psychological dependency. Large quantities can cause coma and death.

Hallucinogens—These are mind-changing drugs and include LSD or "acid." Mescaline and "magic mushrooms" contain similar drugs. They cause "trips," in which the user enters an unreal world, which can be pleasant or terrifying, and can cause the user to behave in an unpredictable manner. Long-term use can cause mental problems.

Designer drugs—These are drugs deliberately designed to produce mood-changing effects. They include "ecstacy," or "E," which can cause a happy feeling leading to hunger and mental problems. Just one tablet has been known to cause sudden death.

IN THE CITY

UNFORTUNATELY, CITIES HAVE a reputation for being less safe places than small towns or the country. So how can we ensure our own personal safety in the city? What can we do to make sure we are not the victim of a theft or an attack? And how can we avoid the dangers of drugs and other harmful substances? There is actually a great deal we can do to enjoy safer lives by following some simple rules.

More crimes take place in the city than elsewhere. There are several reasons for this. Many crimes are easier to commit, and harder to solve, in cities. There are many more people who do not know each other in cities, and so it is harder to identify someone who may have attacked you, for example. There are often richer pickings

Subways
Big city subways (above) can sometimes be dangerous places. If possible, travel with a group of friends. Avoid cars with few people traveling in them, and do not use subways late at night.

Saying "No"
You may be offered all kinds of things in cities like drugs (left), candy, a free ride home, or an invitation to a party. You should refuse offers of drugs, and you must never accept gifts from, or offers to travel with, strangers.

for thieves in cities, too.

We so often seem to hear about the reporting of crimes that we could be forgiven for thinking that nowhere is safe. The reality, however, is that many crimes are confined to certain places or certain times, and the victims are often people who are unaware of how to avoid dangerous situations or who make easy targets.

In many cities police operate a policy called zero tolerance. This means that even small crimes are punished, and this has led to an overall drop in crime. Other measures, such as CCTV (closed circuit television), have meant that crimes can be recorded on camera, making it easier to catch the culprits.

For many people, keeping safe can usually be achieved by following some simple rules and thinking carefully about certain situations in advance.

Dangerous Places

Unfortunately, many places that are perfectly safe by day become less so at night—especially when fewer people are around. Darkness makes it easier for criminals to operate. It is advisable not to travel on public transportation late at night or on your own in the city.

Think ahead. How are you going to get back from, say, a friend's house when it is dark? Would it be better if you arranged for your parents to pick you up? Always make sure you have enough money to buy a ticket if you have no alternative but to travel by public transportation, however.

There are also many other places—parks, city centers, and maybe even parts of your own neighborhood—that you should sometimes avoid. Some places have districts that are considered unsafe for most people even in daytime. Try to find out about these districts, and do not get lost and stray into them by mistake. Keep to the main streets. If you do become lost, seek out a police officer or call for help by dialing 911 (see pages 24–25).

Your Belongings

Keep your belongings safe when you are in the city by following the advice given on page 7.

When It Gets Dark

Like any city park, Central Park, New York (below), can be a place of fun during daylight and when there are plenty of people about. Unfortunately, when night falls, the park is not a safe place for most people and is best avoided.

HIKING AND WALKING

EXPLORING THE GREAT outdoors is fun, but it is always sensible to take a few precautions before going on a trip. Plan your route carefully, and let others know where you are going and what time you intend to return. Make sure that you have some knowledge of the area you are going to, such as the type of terrain and the likely weather. Take plenty of food and the necessary equipment, and wear the right clothing.

Before setting off on any trip—whether it is a hike near your home or an exploration of somewhere new on vacation—the following advice will help you stay safe and enable you to get the maximum enjoyment from the trip.

First, plan your route. If you know the area well, you probably won't need a map; but if you are venturing somewhere new, it is sensible to take a map showing footpaths, potentially dangerous areas like marshes, and other important features.

Make sure you know how to read a map before you set out. You should also know how to use a compass. Compass needles point to north, so you will always know the direction in

Well Prepared

These two young people (right) are well prepared for a walk in the countryside. Their strong outdoor shoes will enable them to cope with rough ground. Each carries a large backpack containing extra clothing, food, and equipment that might be needed in the unlikely event of getting lost.

checklist

Here is a list of the essential items you will need for a trip:

- Warm, waterproof clothing, strong footwear, gloves, and a hat.
- Sunglasses.
- Sunblock.
- First-aid kit.
- Plastic sheet.
- Plenty of food and water.
- Flashlight.
- Whistle—to alert people if you get lost.
- Map.
- Compass.
- Backpack.

If you are planning a longer trip, you will also need:
- Tent.
- Sleeping bag.
- Cooking stove and fuel.
- Matches.
- Cooking utensils.
- Extra food and water.

which you are traveling. When using a map, place the compass on the map, and turn the map until the north-south line marked on the map lines up with the compass needle. This will show you which way around to hold the map. There are also other ways to find your way around; you can read about some of them in books on hiking and exploring the countryside.

Starting Off

Whenever you set off on a trip, always tell someone where you are going and when you expect to return. If you can, go with older, experienced people—

Finding Your Way

It is easy to get lost in woodlands (right). Keep to paths if there are any. A map or a compass is especially useful to help you find your way. Look out for any features— such as streams—that will help you remember the route you want to take. If you are following the same route back, mark the route with stones or piles of twigs at intervals.

especially if you intend to be out after dark. You will need to wear the right clothing, and take some food, water, and safety equipment. The checklist on the left lists the most important items to take on a trip. If the activity is quite challenging, make sure you are fit enough to undertake it.

Check the weather before you set off—newspapers, television, and radio all provide weather forecasts, and there are numbers you can call, too. If the forecast is for poor weather, consider postponing your trip until things improve. When you are out and about, keep a watchful eye on the weather. Different types of clouds,

Emergency Stretcher

Blankets or quilts can be used to make a stretcher, but it will need at least four people to carry it. Roll the edges in to make a tube that can be used as handles. Now gently lift the injured person (right), and move to the required spot. Remember to lower the victim carefully, so that his or her head does not hit the ground.

changes in wind direction and humidity—even natural signs like sheltering animals—can indicate bad weather to come.

There are various sorts of emergencies that can occur on a trip—such as an injury or an illness, a sudden change in the weather, or you are lost. Pages 22–25 and 28–37 explain what steps to take if you are in an emergency situation.

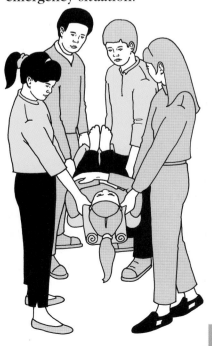

WATER SAFETY

WATER ACTIVITIES ARE usually safe and fun, but it should be remembered that water can also be hazardous. Deep water, currents, tides, offshore winds, and even some aquatic animals can all play their part in creating dangers not only for the unwary swimmer but for anybody using the water for recreation or work. Even strong swimmers can soon find themselves in difficulties—especially when the water is very cold.

Everyone should learn about keeping safe in the water. Events can occur very rapidly in water; one minute you are rowing a boat offshore, and the next it has overturned and you are being

Beach Awareness
Look out for flags and other notices on beaches that tell you when and where it is safe to go in the water. Be sure that the wind and tides are right for sports such as windsurfing, surfing, and bodyboarding (below).

taken out to sea by the tide. Suddenly entering cold water may cause uncontrollable gasping that can lead to water inhalation, a sudden rise in blood pressure, an inability to swim, or hypothermia.

Swimmers should be aware of their own abilities and never get out of their depth unless they can swim well. They should heed all warning signs about tides, etc. Small children must be supervised at all times and never be allowed to float off on inflatable rings or rafts.

Surfers, windsurfers, and other water-sports enthusiasts can usually swim well, too, but they can still get into difficulties if currents or tides take them out to sea. A cold wind can affect tired muscles, making it hard to control a sailboard or even to climb back onto it.

If you intend to explore rock-pools, it is advisable to start at the lowest part of the beach and work your way back up to the top. This will prevent you from becoming cut off by the incoming tide. If you find any-

Pulling from Water
To avoid going into the water yourself, try to find a stick or piece of rope with which you can reach the victim. Lie on the bank as close to the edge as possible, and reach out as shown above.

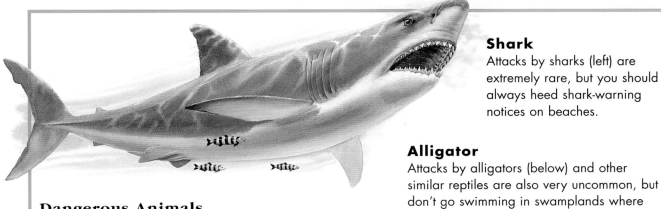

Shark
Attacks by sharks (left) are extremely rare, but you should always heed shark-warning notices on beaches.

Alligator
Attacks by alligators (below) and other similar reptiles are also very uncommon, but don't go swimming in swamplands where they are present.

Dangerous Animals

Although attacks on swimmers by aquatic animals make headlines, they are rare occurrences. Most injuries happen when swimmers get stung by a stingray or a jellyfish, for example. At certain times of year sharks are found in some waters, and in tropical regions some types of cone shells are known to be highly venomous. It is also best to seek advice before swimming in waters that may support snakes or other dangerous reptiles.

thing unusual on the beach—such as canisters washed ashore from a ship—inform the Coast Guard at once. Do not touch anything; it may be dangerous.

Safety on Rivers and Lakes
Many of the rules about safety at sea apply equally to fresh water. If you are in a boat, it is advisable to wear a life jacket even if you can swim. Learn the meanings of the various marker buoys and flags that are used. They indicate, for example, which way to proceed on certain waterways. To ignore them can mean entering unsafe waters or becoming involved in a collision with another vessel.

If you are on foot, beware of steeply shelving banks or marshy areas. Test the depth with a stick first if you are

unsure. Always tell someone where you are going if you intend to go near water.

Drowning
Death by drowning usually occurs because air cannot enter the lungs. This happens when there is water in the lungs, but drowning can also be caused by throat muscles going into spasm.

Someone who has nearly drowned should always receive medical attention. Even if the casualty recovers well, there is a further risk of a condition known as secondary drowning (this is when the air passages begin to swell).

Rescue from Water
If it is necessary to rescue someone from the water, try to do it from the safety of dry land; do not put yourself at risk

while trying to save someone else. Reach out with your hand, a stick, or branch, or throw a rope. If you are trained as a life-saver or if the victim is unconscious, you may have to enter the water to reach him or her. It is safer to wade than to swim. If you cannot reach someone safely, get help immediately.

Treating Drowning
First lay the victim on his or her back. Make sure that nothing is blocking the mouth or throat. Remove wet clothing, and shield the victim from the wind to prevent the body from being chilled further. Place the victim in the recovery position (see page 29), remembering to keep the head low so that water drains from the mouth. Get help so the victim can be taken quickly to a hospital.

FINDING SHELTER FROM THE WEATHER

SOMETIMES ACCIDENTS AND injuries can occur during a hike or ramble, or even when just playing, but the most likely hazard is getting lost or encountering bad weather. In these instances it may be necessary to find shelter until things improve or someone finds you.

Even the best-planned trips can go wrong. You, or perhaps someone who is accompanying you, may get injured by falling or being bitten by an animal, for example. This may make it impossible for you to continue your journey.

Sometimes, particularly in mountainous places, the weather can change suddenly. It can become much colder—perhaps causing snow to fall—or storms, high winds, mist, and rain can make it hard to find your way. In all these situations you may need to shelter until help arrives or you feel well enough to go on.

There are some important rules to follow when you decide to take shelter. **1. Inspection**. Check yourself for injuries such as cuts and bruises, and then check your equipment and clothing to prevent further problems. For example, clothing may need repairing to reduce exposure to the elements. **2. Protection**. Keep yourself warm and dry or out of the sun and wind by building some sort of shelter or by using any available buildings or natural features

like caves. Use backsacks, etc. to provide extra protection. **3. Location**. Find a way of letting rescuers know where you are by leaving something conspicuous for them to see. **4. Food and water**. If rescue seems more than 24 hours away, try to find natural food such as blackberries. Do not eat anything that you cannot be sure is safe. **5. Keep calm**.

Sheltering from the Cold

Try to find some shelter so you do not get wet if it rains or

Beware Lightning

In an electrical storm lightning tends to discharge its electricity on objects that project against the landscape. Isolated trees like these (above) are not the safest place to shelter in a storm, therefore. If you have to shelter under an isolated tree, make sure that you stand several feet away from it and do not touch it.

snows. If you get wet, you will become even colder. Huddle close to companions to retain warmth. Wind can lower tem-

Surviving Outdoors

If you are lost or unable to return due to bad weather, stay where you are, and try to find somewhere warm and dry to shelter until you are rescued or conditions improve. Put on as many layers of clothing as you can, and place your feet in your backpack. Try to find something to sit on so that you are not in contact with the damp ground. Keep your limbs close to your body—this will help retain body heat. Eat some food, and take a warm drink if possible. A plastic sheet with air holes will keep out the cold wind.

something waterproof on top. Or sit with your arms, head, and knees tucked in tightly. If you shelter from a storm, choose dense woods, cliff over-hangs, or hollows in the ground. Do not stand under single trees, on hill tops, near power lines, or in small, isolated buildings. If you shelter by trees, do not touch them but sit crouched as described above.

Finally, note any features or landmarks that may help you find your way back or that could provide shelter if needed. And remember that rescue is just a matter of time.

peratures even more, so always try to get out of the wind. The diagram above shows the best way to keep warm. If you are caught in a snow storm, and there is no shelter from build-ings, etc. it is best to lie in a hollow if you can, so that you are out of the driving wind.

Sheltering from Storms

Storms can blow up suddenly, and it can be dangerous to be caught in one, since you could be struck by lightning. If you are caught in the open, lie face downward on the ground with

Good Shelter

When you are out on a hike, make a mental note of any structures, like this birdwatching blind (right), that you come across. Or if you have a map, make a mark on it to show the location. If you need to shelter, it may be worth retracing your route to get back to such a place.

EMERGENCIES AND GETTING HELP

THE CHIEF THING to remember in an emergency is to get professional help as soon as possible. While waiting for the emergency services to arrive, make the victim comfortable, and prevent him or her from coming to further harm.

An emergency can happen anywhere—in the home, at school, or when traveling. If someone becomes ill or has an accident and is seriously injured, call an ambulance. If there is a fire, call the fire department. And if you see someone getting into difficulties while sailing or swimming in the sea, get in touch with the Coast Guard or alert a lifeguard if there is one patroling the beach. If you are not sure which emergency service to

Heat Exhaustion

If too much water is lost from the body, the victim suffers heat exhaustion. Move him or her to a cool place. Lay the victim down with the legs raised, and help rehydration by giving plenty of water to drink (right).

Heatstroke

Overexposure to heat results in heatstroke. Remove some of the victim's clothes, and pour cold water onto the victim. Then call for a doctor (below).

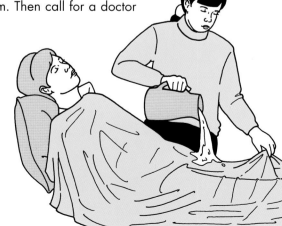

Road Accidents

People injured in a road accident (left) generally need help from the emergency services such as paramedics and, if someone is trapped, the fire department. If you see an accident, make an emergency call to get help as shown below. If there are victims who are out of the vehicle, you may be able to comfort them, but do not put yourself in danger.

The Professionals

Ambulance crews and paramedics (right) are trained to deal with victims of accidents and other emergencies. They know how to give medical treatment and how to move an injured person without the risk of causing further injury.

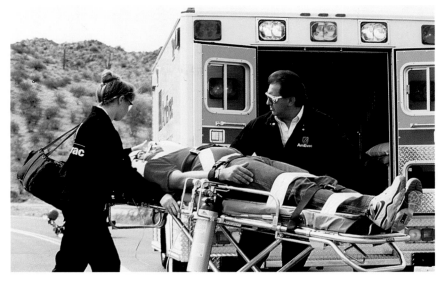

call, just call the police; they will then contact the necessary emergency services. There is more information about keeping safe in the above situations to be found in other parts of this volume.

Many emergencies need the help of paramedics or other professionals. If there is a qualified first-aider on the scene, ask what you can do to help. You may be asked to call for help (see below) or may be asked to help keep curious people from crowding around and getting in the first-aider's way.

Making Emergency Calls

Unless you have a mobile telephone, quickly find a public phone. Dial 911 (this is a toll-free call). An operator will ask

which service you need (this information is given at the beginning of this section). Keep calm and talk clearly. When you have been connected to the emergency service, they will need some information:
• Your telephone number.
• The location of the incident (building, road name, number).

• The type of incident (road traffic accident, fire, etc.).
• The number of victims.
• The condition of the victims.
• Any hazards (such as damaged power lines, gasoline on the road, etc.).
Do not disconnect the call to the emergency services unless they tell you to do so.

Hypothermia

Hypothermia occurs when the body temperature drops. It can happen indoors in poorly heated conditions as well as outdoors. It is common in old people and sometimes infants. The signs are shivering, looking pale, feeling cold to the touch, and looking drowsy. If indoors, wrap the victim in a blanket (right) and give them a warm drink and some chocolate. Outdoors, hypothermia can be caused by exposure, wet or windy conditions, illness, and alcohol. Wrap the victim in a blanket or something warm, and try to get him or her somewhere warmer.

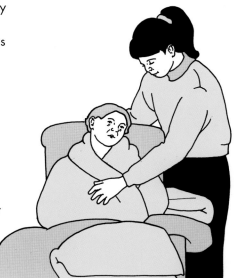

FIRE SAFETY

FIRES ARE ALWAYS potentially dangerous situations. A small fire can often spread quickly and become a major inferno, causing property damage, injury, and even death. Never put yourself in danger when trying to extinguish a fire or help a victim. If you cannot put a fire out quickly, you must leave the area as fast as possible and then telephone the emergency services, giving as much information as you can.

Fires can start for a variety of different reasons, including faulty electrical appliances, sparks from fires, and cooking accidents. All fires need three basic components: **ignition** (such as a spark); **fuel** (such as gasoline, fabric, wood, or paper); and **oxygen** (present in the air). Every year about 2.5 million fires are reported to fire departments in the United States. It is important to know how to prevent fires, how to avoid danger if there is a fire, how to help a victim, and how to get the emergency services.

Local fire departments inspect public buildings regularly to check for fire hazards, and firefighters give demonstrations at schools to teach about fire dangers. Your school will rehearse what to do in case of fire by holding fire drills. Make sure you know the fire drill, the exits you should leave the buildings by and the asssembly points, and listen to any special instructions you are given.

General Fire Safety

Many fires are avoidable if a few safety rules are followed:

Fire Extinguishers

There are several different types of fire extinguisher available, and each is designed to be used on a particular sort of fire. Carbon dioxide extinguishers (1) are for use only on fires involving flammable liquids or gases and electricity. Dry powder extinguishers (2) are for general purpose use. They smother flames. Soda-acid extinguishers (3) squirt water onto fires involving materials like wood and paper. They must not be used on electrical fires. The fire triangle (left) shows the three components necessary for a fire to start. Fire extinguishers attack one or more of these components, putting the fire out.

• Never play with fire or matches.
• Always keep a guard around an open-hearth fire, and make sure it is safe to leave unattended.
• Make sure nothing is so close to a fire that it could ignite.
• Do not stand too close to bonfires or fireworks.
• Avoid hot fat catching fire in the kitchen.

• Do not use faulty electrical appliances.

If There Is a Fire

If a fire alarm sounds at school or in a public place you should observe the fire drill and leave the area immediately. In public places follow signs for fire exits if you hear fire alarms. Do not use elevators or escalators; use

Smoke and Fumes

If you become trapped in a burning building, find a room with a window and close the door. Place a blanket or coat against the bottom of the door to stop the smoke from entering. Open the window and call for help (below). If you go through a smoke-filled room to escape, keep low to the floor since there is more oxygen, and it is also cooler at ground level.

Fire-safe House

Many homes now also have fire-prevention devices built in (below).

stairs. If a fire occurs at other times and you cannot put it out easily, you should again leave the area immediately and call the emergency services (see pages 24–25). *Never put yourself at risk when trying to put out a fire*. If you have to leave a building, alert everyone else in the building first, if safe to do so. Close all doors behind you. Look for fire exits and meeting points; wait in this area until it is safe for you to leave.

Dealing with Fire

If the fire is small, it may be possible for you to extinguish it. Fires involving wood, such as campfires and bonfires, can be put out using plenty of water. Never pour water onto an electrical fire—use a fire extinguisher designed for the purpose. Fires involving hot oil, such as a burning frying pan, can be put out using a fireproof blanket or a towel drenched in water. Turn

any cooking appliances off before putting out the fire.

In a confined space a fire will use up oxygen as it burns. Never enter a smoke-filled building or open a door leading to a fire or smoke, since there may not be sufficient oxygen to breathe. There may also be dangerous fumes from burning materials.

Helping Fire Victims

If someone has been overcome by smoke or fumes, try to get him or her into fresh air so that breathing becomes easier. It may be possible for you to douse them or their clothes with cold water if they are smoldering or burning. Lay the victim down with the burns uppermost before you do this. Minor burns can be treated by following the advice given on page 31.

If you know how, use the technique described on page 29 to restore breathing if necessary. As soon as you can, get help by calling the emergency services.

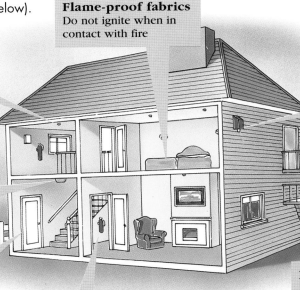

Flame-proof fabrics
Do not ignite when in contact with fire

Sprinkler
Automatically squirts water onto a fire once it has started

Fire alarm
Alerts the fire-fighting services

Smoke detector
Emits a piercing alarm to alert you

Fire-proof doors
Close automatically and prevent fire from spreading

Fire escape
Allows you to leave safely

Fire extinguisher
Fights fires

BREATHING PROBLEMS

WHEN WE BREATHE through either our nose or mouth, air enters our windpipe and travels down to the lungs. This happens automatically, so we do not have to think about it. Problems arise when something obstructs the airway, and we are unable to take in air. The body will try automatically to remove the obstruction by coughing. Sometimes, however, we need help to clear the obstruction.

Breathing problems can be caused by a number of things. There may be an object—such as candy—stuck in a person's throat that is blocking the airway and causing the victim to choke. Breathing difficulties may also be caused by panic attacks (see *Personality and Behavior*, page 33) or asthma (see page 29 and *Health and Illness*, page 19).

Breathing problems can be very serious, so get help immediately if someone is showing any of the signs listed in the checklist below or is unconscious.

checklist

Look out for the following signs of someone with breathing problems:
- **Victim has difficulty speakng and breathing.**
- **Victim may be grasping at his or her neck.**
- **Victim's skin may be a blue-gray color due to a lack of oxygen.**
- **Victim may point at his or her throat to indicate problem.**

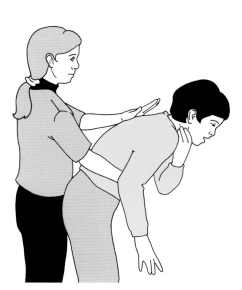

Choking

Choking requires quick action, since the victim may collapse and stop breathing. Choking in adults is usually caused by food that has not been chewed or swallowed correctly, although fluids can sometimes cause choking as well.

A child can choke very easily, and care should be taken to make sure that small children do not put objects in their mouths that could block the airway. For the same reason it is also important that children do not have food in their mouths when running and playing.

Choking Child

If someone seems to be choking get him or her to bend forward as shown (above left), and then give five sharp slaps between the shoulder blades with your open hand while asking the victim to cough. If this treatment fails to remove the object, make a fist with one of your hands and hold it against the victim's abdomen just below the ribs as shown above. Now hold the fist with your other hand. Press into the victim's abdomen and pull up sharply four or five times to remove the object. The victim must then go to see a doctor or go to hospital to be checked out.

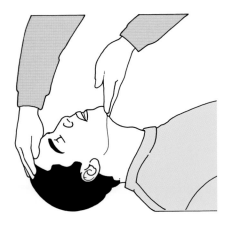

Opening the Airway

Help the victim is by lifting his or her chin and tilting the head, which pulls the tongue away from the throat and opens the airway (above). Kneel beside the person about level with his or her shoulder. Place two fingers under the point of the chin with one hand, and place the other hand on their forehead. Gently tilt the head back (above). If you think the victim has hurt his or her neck, you must handle the head very carefully.

Hyperventilation

If someone becomes anxious or has a panic attack, they may start breathing too fast and too deeply. This increases the oxygen in the circulatory system and can cause dizziness, fainting, trembling, and cramps. You can help restore normal breathing for the victim by taking him or her to a quiet place and asking them to breath into, and out of, a paper bag. This lets the victim breathe air that he or she has just breathed out, which has less oxygen in it.

Asthma

This condition is becoming increasingly common in young people. It makes the muscles in the air passages contract, reducing the airway and making it difficult to breathe. Asthma attacks can be triggered by dust, pollen, food allergies, tablets, smoke, or animals.

Asthma victims usually

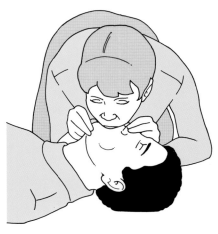

Mouth-to-mouth Resuscitation

This is how this life-saving technique is done (above). After the airway is opened, the soft part of the victim's nose is pinched closed. Then the first-aider takes a deep breath, places his or her lips over the victim's mouth, and blows for two seconds. The victim's chest is allowed to fall for four seconds before the sequence is repeated. If a pulse is felt, mouth-to-mouth resuscitation is continued at a rate of ten breaths per minute. Then the pulse is checked again. At this stage the paramedics will be called for. If there is no pulse, the paramedics will use other procedures to get the victim to begin breathing.

control the condition with their own medication. Keep the person calm and comfortable. Help him or her take the medication and encourage the victim to breath deeply and slowly. This should ease the breathing after about five minutes. If it is the person's first attack, he or she gets worse, or the medication has no effect, get medical help.

Recovery Position

Open and check the airway. If you can see anything stuck in the throat, try to carefully remove it. Check the victim's pockets and remove any fragile or bulky objects. Now carefully turn the victim onto his or her side to lie as shown below. The foot of one leg should be level with the knee of the other leg. Notice how the hand on the same side as the bent leg is placed under the victim's cheek. Once the victim is in this position, tilt the head back **slightly to open the airway again.**

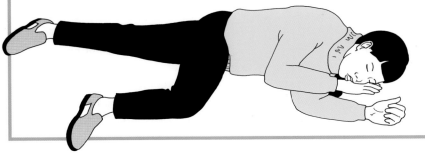

CUTS, SCRAPES, SCALDS, AND BURNS

THERE ARE SOME common injuries that most of us get from time to time. Fortunately, most of them are not serious, and the advice here will help ease the condition. More serious wounds, or pains that persist, should be checked out by a doctor as soon as possible.

When the skin is broken because of a wound, blood is lost from the body. This is known as external bleeding. If the skin does not get broken but blood is still lost from vessels, it is known as internal bleeding.

Nosebleeds

Nosebleeds can be caused by blood vessels in the nose being ruptured, usually by a blow or as a result of high blood pressure.

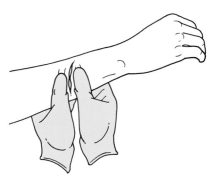

Severe Bleeding

Squeeze the wound edges together to minimize the blood loss (above). Place the limb higher than the heart to also reduce the blood loss. Place a pad lightly over the wound and secure in place with a bandage. Get the victim to a hospital as soon as possible.

Nosebleeds

Get the victim to sit down and lean forward so that the blood is not swallowed. Ask the victim to pinch the soft part of his or her nose, which will help the blood clot. After ten minutes release the pressure from the nose. If bleeding starts again, apply pressure for a further ten minutes.

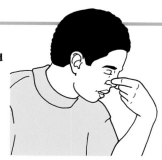

Mouth Bleeds

Bleeding from the mouth can result from a cut to the tongue, lips, or lining of the mouth, which can be caused by the victim's own teeth or a blow to the mouth. As with nosebleeds, get the victim to sit down and lean forward so that the blood drains from the mouth. Place a pad over the wound, and press for ten minutes.

To stop a nosebleed, apply the technique described above. When the nosebleed has stopped, tell the victim not to pick, blow, or squeeze their nose for 24 hours.

Mouth Bleeds

Bleeding from the mouth can result from a cut to the tongue, lips, or the lining of the mouth. These can be caused by the person's own teeth, a blow to the mouth, or something sharp being put in the mouth. Treat the wound as described above.

Head Wounds

Head wounds are very serious, since the brain can become damaged. The skin may also tear, causing a wound and loss of blood. The victim must go to hospital for treatment.

Embedded Objects

An embedded object can result from an accident in the home or garden. It can include pieces of glass (from falling into a

Cooling a Burn

As soon as possible, cool the burn with cold running water for at least ten minutes (above). This will stop the burn extending through the body and will ease the pain. Try to lay the victim down and raise his or her legs to minimize the shock.

door), sharp twigs and branches, or even tools in the garden. Do not try to remove the object, but seek medical help as soon as possible.

Severe Bleeding

Wounds to the trunk (chest), abdomen (below the chest), or legs can cause serious bleeding since they are large areas with a rich blood supply. Follow the instructions on page 30 to deal with severe bleeding.

Burns

When someone has been burned, try to find out what caused it. You may need to tell the hospital so that they can give the correct treatment.

If the victim's airway has been affected, it may cause breathing difficulties. If this is the case, a first-aider may need to give mouth-to-mouth resuscitation (see page 29).

Types of Burn

A **superficial burn** is the least serious burn. It usually affects only the outermost skin area.

A **partial-thickness burn** usually causes blisters when it burns the skin.

A **full-thickness burn** is the most severe type. It burns the underlyimg nerve, fat, and muscle tissues.

How Burns and Scalds Are Caused

• Scald—hot liquids, fat, and steam.
• Dry burn—cigarettes and rope burns.
• Electrical burn—low- or high-voltage currents, power cables, and lightning strikes.
• Cold burn—liquid oxygen or

nitrogen and frostbite.
• Chemical burn—paint stripper, bleach, acid, and alkali.
• Radiation burn—X-rays and sunshine.

Treating Burns and Scalds

All treatment for burns and scalds by the first-aider is aimed at stopping the burning, reducing infection, and relieving pain. The most effective treatment for the first-aider is to quickly cool the burn with plenty of cold water (see above), dress the burn if necessary, and get the victim to a hospital for further treatment.

checklist

• Do not place yourself in danger when helping a burn victim.
• Do not remove any sticking clothing since this will remove the skin as well.
• Do not touch the affected area with your hands.
• Do not break blisters.
• Do not apply creams or lotions to the burned area since they will have to be removed at a hospital.

Improvised Bandages

If you do not have a first-aid kit available, you can make an improvised bandage (1–3, right). Do not use fluffy materials, but use items such as pillowcases, scarves, and dish towels. Your aim is to stop the bleeding; when the injured person gets to a hospital, all dressings will be removed so that the wound can be treated.

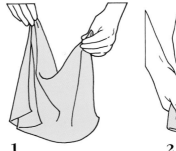

1

2

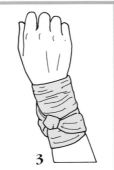

3

MUSCLE AND BONE INJURIES

MUSCLE INJURIES CAN range from sprains and pulls to more serious tearing of the tissues. Ligaments and tendons can also get sprained or torn. Bone injuries normally result in a breakage, or fracture, that may require surgery in order to help reset the bone.

Muscles are attached to bones by tendons. The joints are supported by sheaths of connective tissue called ligaments (see *The Human Body*, pages 10–11). Because muscles and bones are connected, an injury to one can sometimes cause an injury to the other.

Sprains

A sprain is an injury to the ligament (the tissue that supports bones around joints) caused by a sudden wrenching movement at the joint. It can be caused, for example, when the ankle is twisted by landing awk-wardly (see *Health and Illness*, page 25). The ligament is often torn in such an injury.

Tendons (as well as the muscles themselves) can also be torn, causing internal bleeding.

Strains

A strain can occur when the muscle is overstretched. It can again cause internal bleeding. This injury is commonly caused when you exercise while your muscles are cold—for example, if you sprint hard before warming up first.

The treatment for sprains and strains is the same. The injured part is placed in a position that is comfortable for the person. A cold compress—a towel soaked in cold water and then wrung out—or an ice pack (crushed

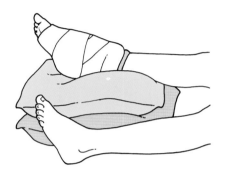

Sprains and Strains

The victim's limb is raised to reduce swelling, using either an item of furniture or the first-aider's knee for support. The affected area is cooled with an ice pack (a pack of frozen vegetables makes a useful emergency ice pack) for ten minutes and then removed. The area is then surrounded with soft padding and secured with a bandage (above). The limb is kept raised while a doctor checks out the injury.

Broken Bones

If someone has an open fracture, a first-aider will cover the wound with a dressing and apply gentle pressure to help prevent bleeding (left). If the victim has a closed fracture, the limb will be held still to stop further injury. In both cases the person should be taken to a hospital quickly.

ice wrapped in a cloth) is placed over the injured area, and the injured limb is raised. This will reduce bruising and swelling and ease the pain. If the sprain or strain is severe, the casualty must go to a hospital. If it is a minor injury, the victim will be advised to rest and to see their doctor (see also *Health and Illness*, page 25).

Broken Bones

Even though bones are tough and resilient, they can be fractured (broken) by a heavy blow or dislocated (pulled from their sockets) by a violent twist. If the bone breaks through the skin, it is called an open, or compound, fracture. If the skin remains intact, it is called a closed fracture (see *Health and Illness,* page 24).

If you think someone has a broken limb, do not move the victim or the broken limb unnecessarily, since this may cause further injury and may be very painful. Steady and support the injured limb with either your hand or, if the broken limb is an arm, by placing it in a sling (see right). This will help protect it and keep it still. Get help as soon as possible.

Dressings and Bandages

Dressings are prepacked, sterile materials that are placed onto wounds such as cuts and scrapes (see pages 30–31) to help prevent blood loss and to keep the wound free from infection. They consist of a piece of gauze attached to a bandage and are available in many sizes. Wherever possible, a dressing is used to cover a wound in order to prevent infection and reduce blood loss.

The main purpose of a bandage is to hold a dressing in place. It can also be used to control bleeding and to help reduce swelling.

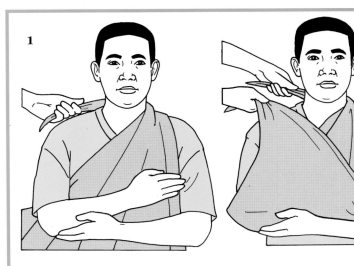

Putting on a Sling

The victim's injured arm is placed across his or her chest in the most comfortable position, and it is supported with the other hand. One end of a large bandage is slid underneath the injured arm and opened out; the top end is brought over the shoulder (1). The lower end of the bandage is brought up and over the shoulder and tied with a reef knot on the injured side (2). Both ends of the bandage are tucked under the knot.

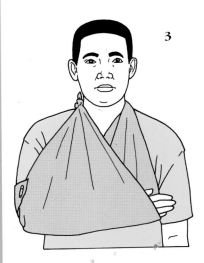
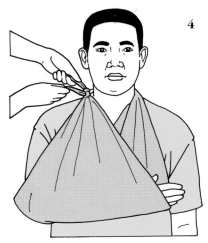

The part of the bandage near the elbow should be pinned to the front using a safety pin (3). This will secure the elbow in place and acts as a corner for the sling. If the first aider does not have a safety pin, the flap can be tucked into the corner of the sling. The circulation should be checked regularly. If necessary, the sling should be undone and tied in a more comfortable position (4). The arm should not be moved around too much while doing this.

BITES AND STINGS

Insects and other animals do not usually attack unless provoked, injured, or placed in a situation that frightens them—such as being cornered or accidentally stepped on. Most of the time they try to avoid humans if they can. Bites and stings often occur when we are on vacation or when out in the countryside, but in some areas snakes and spiders in particular can be found in the home.

Most animal stings cause discomfort, but they can often be treated with simple first aid. Animal bites are usually more serious, however, and may carry with them the added danger of infections entering the body.

Snake Bites

There are many poisonous snakes in the warmer parts of the world. The United States has several dangerous species—such as the rattlesnake, the harlequin coral snake, and the water moccasin—and you must be extra careful when entering

Rattlesnake

Adder

an area where they might live. Most snake bites occur because someone has frightened a snake or accidentally stepped on it. If you see a snake, just leave it undisturbed and move away.

If someone has been bitten, try to reassure the victm and keep him or her calm while you get help. An overexcited victim's heart rate will speed up, circulating the poison more quickly.

Other Animal Bites

If an animal bites, the teeth can cause deep puncture wounds that will carry germs into the body. This can cause a reaction

Snake Bites

Try to reassure the victim and keep him or her calm. Lay the victim down so that the bite area is lower than the heart—this will prevent the poison from circulating so quickly. Get help as soon as possible. Two poisonous snakes that are sometimes encountered are shown left.

known as anaphylactic shock.

Anaphylactic shock is a condition in which the victim suffers a major allergic reaction to a poison. Their blood pressure will fall, and breathing will become difficult. The skin will appear to be red and blotchy, and the neck and face may swell. A person showing these symptoms must be taken to a hospital quickly, so you should get help as soon as possible.

Insect Stings

When wasps, bees, and hornets sting, the affected area will become painful, red, and swollen. It is rarely dangerous, but anaphylactic shock may develop (see above), which is very serious. If the person has

fact file

The world's most poisonous creature is the box jelly—a kind of jellyfish. The box jelly lives in the waters off the coast of Australia.

The rattlesnake rattles the scales on the end of its tail as a warning to keep away.

A bee can only sting once; a wasp can sting many times.

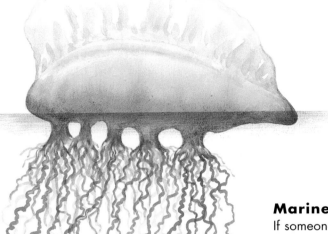

Spider Bites

Some spiders, such as the black widow (right), are extremely poisonous. If someone has been bitten by a spider, follow the instructions opposite for treating snake bites.

Marine Animal Stings

If someone has been stung by a poisonous fish, jellyfish, or Portuguese man-of-war (left), sit them down, reassure them, and wash the affected area with vinegar, if available, or with sea water. This will help reduce the effect of the venom. Cases of severe stinging should be treated by a doctor.

suffered multiple stings, the throat and airway may become swollen, and help must be sought as soon as possible.

The stings of other animals—such as some scorpions—may be more serious because the poison is very strong, and medical help should be sought if someone is stung.

Marine Animal Stings

Marine animals such as the Portuguese man-of-war, sea anemones, and jellyfish pass on their venom through stinging cells on their tentacles. If you see jellyfish or similar creatures floating in the sea, get out of the water. Wear something on your feet when wading in rock pools to avoid being stung by sea anemones.

First Aid for Bites

Bleeding wounds are usually first cleaned and covered with a dressing that is secured in place with a bandage (below). If you are bitten by an animal, such as a dog, you should go to a hospital for a tetanus injection in order to prevent a blood infection.

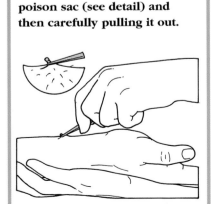

Treating Stings

If the sting is still in the wound, try to wash it away with water. Someone may be able to remove the sting by grasping it with tweezers just below the poison sac (see detail) and then carefully pulling it out.

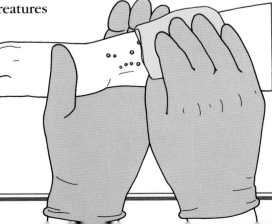

MISCELLANEOUS AILMENTS

THERE ARE SOME minor conditions that many of us suffer from occasionally. It is usually a straightforward matter to ease the discomfort of these common aches and pains. Medical help should always be sought if any ailments continue to cause pain.

Miscellaneous ailments describe the various conditions that many of us suffer from occasionally. Often these conditions can develop quickly and can be unpleasant, although many may be prevented from becoming worse if treated quickly. These are the most common ones.

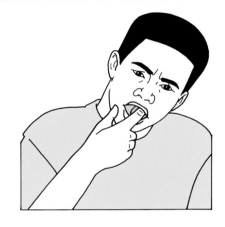

Toothache
Most people can tolerate a mild toothache, but sometimes a tooth can be very painful. This can be caused by a decaying tooth or an infection in the gums. The condition can be made worse by either hot or cold drinks, eating food, or brushing your teeth too hard.

Toothache
To ease the pain of a toothache, place a warm hot-water bottle, wrapped in a towel, on the victim's face. Place the person in the position most comfortable for him or her. As soon as possible, arrange an appointment to see a dentist. Holding a piece of absorbent cotton soaked in clove oil against the tooth (left) may help.

Cramps
This condition is often very painful and is caused by the muscles going suddenly into a

Cramps
To relieve bouts of cramps, gently massage the area and slowly stretch the muscle after each spasm has passed. Repeat until the cramp has disappeared. For foot cramps, get the victim to put his or her weight on the front of the foot first until the spasm has passed.

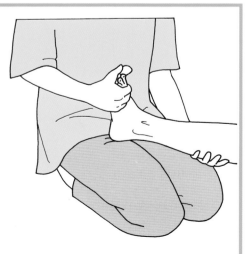

fact file

Our normal body temperature is 98.6°F (37°C). Certain conditions, such as earache, may cause a rise in body temperature. Call a doctor if it rises above 104°F (40°C).

Some conditions, such as headaches, can be symptoms of more serious illnesses such as influenza, poisoning, or meningitis.

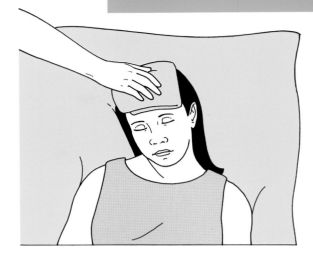

Earache

If the pain is severe, the victim should see a doctor as soon as possible. If the pain is mild, place the person in a comfortable position. Ease the pain by placing a warm hot-water bottle, wrapped in a towel, on his or her ear (above). If the pain persists, call a doctor.

Headache

Help the victim to sit or lie down in a quiet room with no loud distractions, and apply a cold compress (above). If possible, keep lighting low, and make sure the person has plenty of fresh air. If the pain does not go away, seek medical advice as soon as possible.

spasm (in other words, they contract involuntarily). This may occur when the person is asleep, but can happen after exercise when salt and fluids are lost through sweating.

Earache

Earache can be caused by colds, influenza, an infection such as a boil, or by something in the ear. The condition can cause partial or total hearing loss.

Headache

Headaches can be caused by colds, stuffy or smoke-filled atmospheres, stress, tiredness, alcohol, or drugs. Headaches also sometimes occur as a result of something more serious, such as a head injury. If the victim has had a fall or a blow to the head, he or she should see a doctor as soon as possible.

There are other conditions that will need medical help immediately. They are when the pain is severe, when it occurred quickly and for no reason, when the person also suffers a stiff neck, or when the person suffers from loss of feeling to a limb or even unconsciousness.

Hiccups

The easiest way to cure a bout of hiccups is to get the victim to place a paper bag over the nose and mouth and ask him or her to breath normally (right). This will result in the person breathing in air that has just been breathed out, which will contain higher carbon dioxide levels than fresh air.

Hiccups

This is caused by the diaphragm (the sheet of muscle above the abdomen) going into a spasm. This causes the windpipe to partially close, causing the repeated hiccups. The problem usually lasts only a few minutes.

GLOSSARY

Absorption The uptake of a fluid or gas by the body across cell membranes.

Accident An unexpected or unplanned event that may result in damage or harm.

Amphetamine A type of drug that is sometimes used as a stimulant.

Anaphylactic shock A dangerous condition in which the victim suffers a major allergic reaction to a substance; it can be triggered by certain drugs, poisons, or foods. Symptoms include a drop in blood pressure, a blotchy skin, and difficulty in breathing.

Asthma A narrowing of the breathing tubes, or bronchi, in the lungs, causing wheezing, coughs, and shortness of breath.

Barbiturate A chemical compound that, under medical supervision, can be used for sedation or to encourage sleep.

Bite A cut, puncture, or wound to the body caused by the teeth or jaws of another animal.

Burn An injury to the tissues in a part of the body, such as the skin or muscles, caused by heat, extreme cold, or by coming into contact with certain chemicals.

Canister A sealed container—usually a type of drum or can—containing a substance.

Choking A potentially serious condition in which the windpipe is blocked—for example, by food—and the victim coughs violently to try to clear the obstruction.

Contact sport Any sport that involves physical contact with one or more opponents.

Corrosive substance A chemical that can cause burning when in contact with the body; corrosive chemicals include some acids and alkalis.

Depressant A substance that lowers the level of one or more of the body's activities.

Detergent A substance used for cleaning purposes; some detergents can be poisonous.

Discomfort An unpleasant feeling or mild pain.

Drug When given under medical supervision, a drug is a chemical substance used for preventing or curing a disease or illness. Some drugs are used illegally to produce feelings such as relaxation or excitement in the user.

Embedded object A foreign object that is fixed firmly in the body and either protruding out from it or projecting into it.

Emergency A dangerous situation that requires sudden and urgent action.

Exhaustion The condition in which a person is lacking completely in mental or physical energy.

Extinguish To put out (for example, a fire).

First aid The act of giving immediate medical assistance to a victim before the arrival of a doctor or other qualified persons.

Flammable substance One that is easily set on fire.

Gasping Taking short, sudden breaths; the condition is often caused by physical or mental shock.

Gun cabinet A strong, securely locked cabinet used for the safe storage of weapons and ammunition.

Hallucinogen A chemical or drug that causes illusions in the mind.

Hazardous substance Any substance that is harmful if it comes into contact with the body.

Heat exhaustion A condition caused by the body losing too much water.

Heatstroke A condition caused by overexposure to high temperatures.

Hyperventilation A condition in which the victim breathes at a quick and very deep rate, causing too much oxygen to enter the body.

Hypothermia A condition in which the body temperature drops to a dangerously low level, and the victim becomes very cold.

Infection An invasion of the body by foreign organisms such as bacteria or viruses, causing disease or illness.

Inhalation The act of breathing in, or inhaling.

Intermingling The mixing together of objects.

Marker buoy An anchored float that is used to give information to vessels traveling on water; for example, warning of submerged rocks.

Medicine Any substance that is used to treat a disease or cure an illness. Many medicines can be dangerous if they are used incorrectly.

Meningitis An infection of the meninges—the membranes that surround the brain and spinal cord—leading to a high fever and neck stiffness.

Mouth-to-mouth resuscitation A form of first-aid treatment in which the first-aider breathes into the victim's mouth or nose in order to put oxygen into the lungs.

Mugging An attack on a person with the intention to rob.

Narcotic Any of the class of drugs known as opiates that can dull the senses, relieve pain, or induce drowsiness. An overdose can lead to death.

Paramedic A professionally trained person who is qualified to give first aid and medical treatment when necessary.

Passport An official document that gives the holder of the passport permission to visit foreign countries and provides proof of his or her identity.

Poison Any substance that can cause illness or death.

Pollution The poisoning of the natural environment.

Quarry The site of an excavation in the ground, especially to extract rocks and other minerals.

Recovery position The safe position in which to place a victim who is unconscious; it maintains the airway by keeping the head low and allowing the chest to move freely.

Rehydration A form of treatment in which a victim is given sufficient water to restore body fluids after he or she has been dehydrated (has lost fluids from the body).

Safety The condition in which a person is free from harm or danger.

Spasm A condition in which some of the muscles contract involuntarily for a period of time—for example, when a person suffers from cramps.

Stimulant A substance that raises the level of one or more of the body's activities.

Sting A small puncture hole made in the skin by an animal such as a wasp, or a plant such as a stinging nettle, with the intention of injecting a poison into the body.

Tide The regular, twice-daily movement of water on a beach or in an estuary.

Tranquilizer A drug that has a calming effect on the body.

Unconsciousness The potentially serious condition in which a person is unaware of their surroundings and appears to be asleep but cannot be roused normally.

Underpass A road, street, or path that goes underneath another.

Venom The poisonous fluid that some animals—such as certain snakes, insects, and jellyfish—inject into their victims by stinging or biting them.

Venomous Possessing venom.

Visa An official notification—usually in the form of a document or a stamp made in a passport—that a country is allowing a person from another country to enter.

INDEX

FURTHER READING

Ardley, Neil. *Language and Communication.* Franklin Watts, 1992.

Bramwell, Martin. *The Environment and Conservation.* Prentice Hall, 1992.

Bryan, Jenny. *The History of Health and Medicine.* Thomson Learning, 1996.

Byczynski, Lynn. *Genetics: Nature's Blueprints.* Lucent Books, 1991.

Cochrane, Kerry. *The Internet.* Franklin Watts, 1995.

Facchini, Firoenzo. *Humans; Origin and Evolution.* Steck-Vaughn, 1995.

Feldman, Robert S. *Understanding Stress.* Franklin Watts, 1992.

Jukes, Mavis. *It's a Girl Thing: How to Stay Safe, Healthy, and in Charge.* Knopf, 1996.

Kaufman, Gershen and Raphael, Lev. *Stick Up For Yourself: Every Kid's Guide to Personal Power and Positive Self Esteem.* Free Spirit Publishers, 1990.

Kincher, Jonni and Bach, Julie S. (editors). *Psychology for Kids:*

40 Fun Tests That Help You Learn about Yourself. Free Spirit Publishers, 1995.

Krulick, Nancy E. *Don't Stress! How to Keep Life's Problems Little.* Scholastic Trade, 1998.

Lambert, Mark. *Farming and the Environment.* Steck-Vaughn, 1991.

Madison, Arnold. *Drugs and You,* revised ed. Messner, 1990.

Morris, Charles G. *Psychology: An Introduction,* 7th ed. Prentice Hall, 1990.

Reef, Catherine. *Think Positive; Cope with Stress.* Twenty-first Century Books, 1995.

Sanders, Pete, Myers, Steve, and Lacey, Mike. *Relationships (What Do You Know About).* Copper Beech Books, 1998.

Smith, Tony. *The Human Body.* Dorling Kindersley, 1995.

Tessar, Jenny. *Humans.* Blackbirch, 1994.

Wescott, Nadine Bernard. *The Care and Keeping of Friends.* Pleasant Company Publishers, 1996.

Wright, David. *Computers.* Benchmark Books, 1995.